Mel Bay Presents

Easy Classics for **VIOLIN**

With Piano Accompaniment

Piano Accompaniments
by **Jannette Spitzer**
and **Laura Spitzer**

Selected and Arranged
by **Peter Spitzer**

The *Easy Classics* books were written to provide beginning to intermediate instrumentalists with an enjoyable introduction to some of the great classic melodies.

The flute, clarinet, alto sax, tenor sax, and trumpet parts are fully compatible, and may be played in any combination, with or without piano accompaniment. (Note to the pianist: Solo and duet parts are shown in the upper staff, in concert key. For some instruments, actual pitch may be in a lower octave.)

The violin book is transposed to keys suitable for that instrument, and has its own accompaniment.

Peter Spitzer

Contents

Ode to Joy
from Symphony #9

Moderato

Ludwig van Beethoven (1770-1827)

3

Sleeping Beauty Waltz
from the ballet "Sleeping Beauty"

Peter Ilich Tchaikovsky (1843-1890)

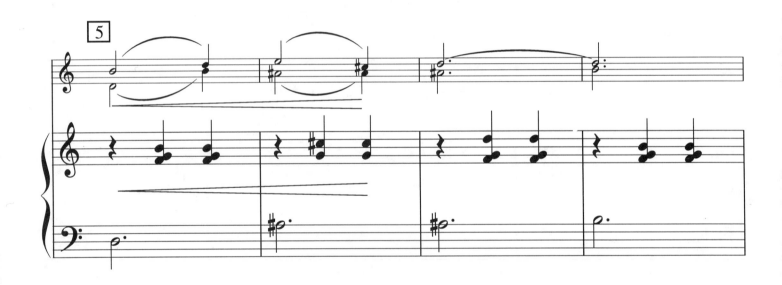

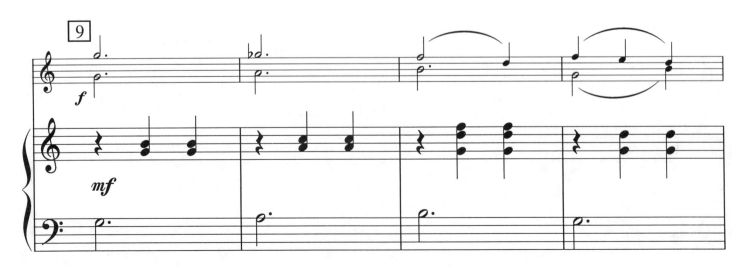

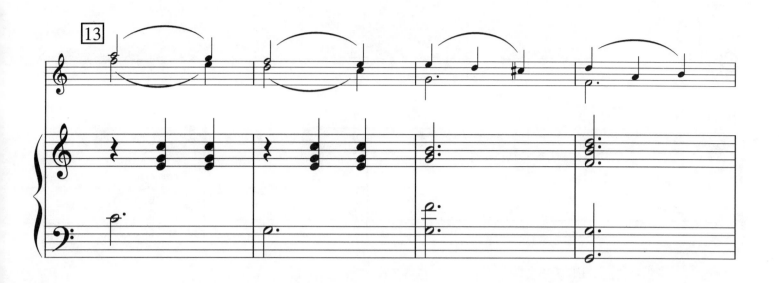

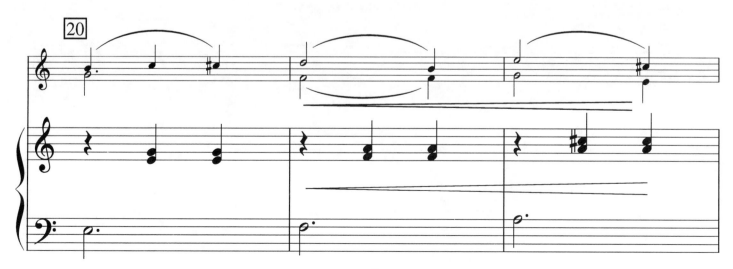

vln. 1 opt. 8va

Eine Kleine Nachtmusik

from Serenade K. 525

Allegro moderato

Wolfgang Amadeus Mozart (1756-1791)

Adagio
from Clarinet Concerto, K. 622

Wolfgang Amadeus Mozart (1756-1791)

Hungarian Dance #5

Johannes Brahms (1833-1897)

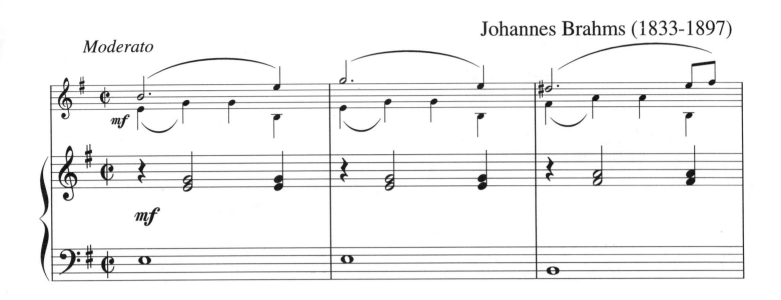

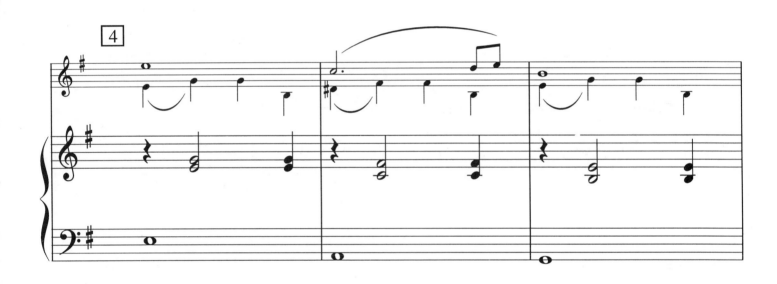

13

Emperor Hymn

Franz Joseph Haydn (1732-1809)

15

The Trout

Franz Schubert (1797-1828)

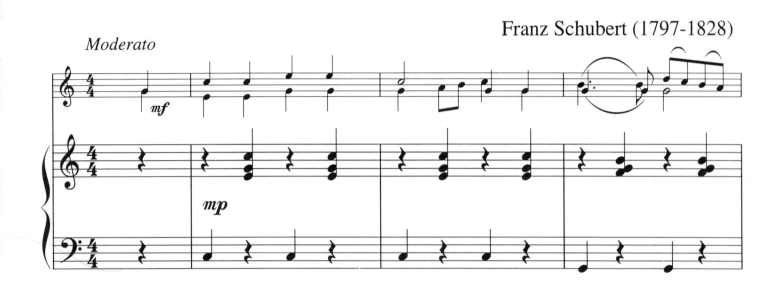

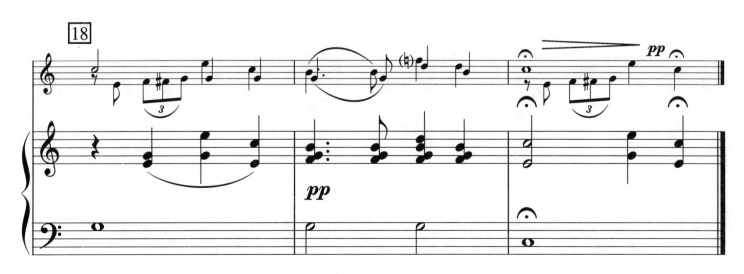

Theme from Polovetsian Dances

from the opera "Prince Igor"

Alexander Borodin (1833-1887)

19

Scheherazade

21

Jesu, Joy of Man's Desiring
from Cantata No. 147

Johann Sebastian Bach (1685-1750)

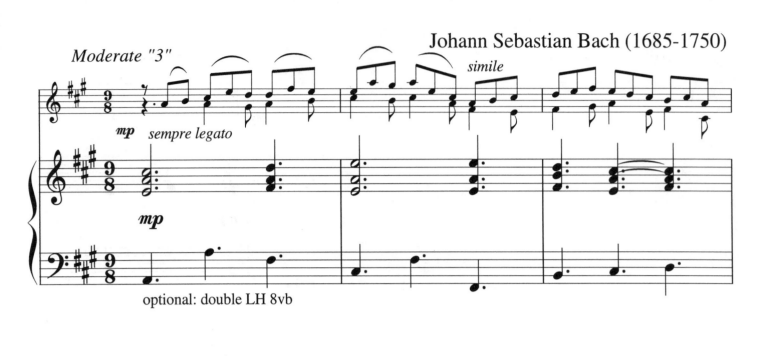

Radetzky March

Johann Strauss (1804-1849)

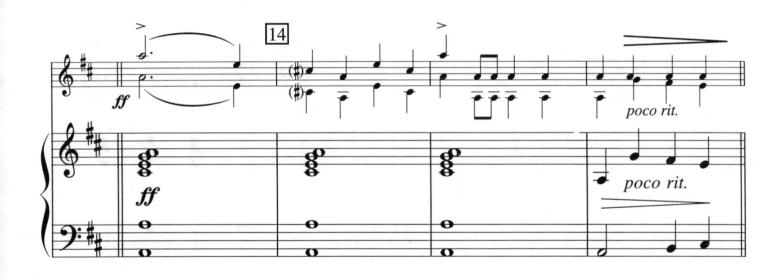

Cancan

from the opera "Orpheus in the Underworld"

Allegro

Jacques Offenbach (1819-1880)

Habanera

from the opera "Carmen"

Georges Bizet (1838-1875)

Toreador Song
from the opera "Carmen"

Georges Bizet (1838-1875)

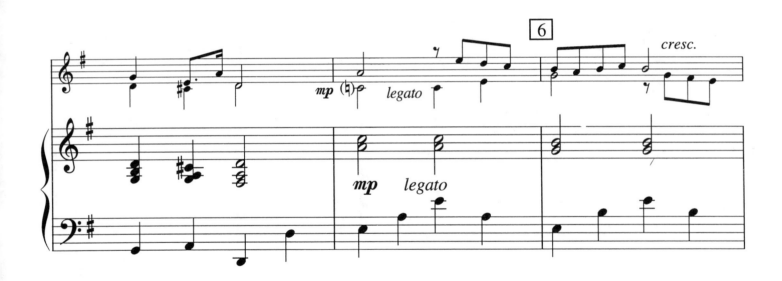

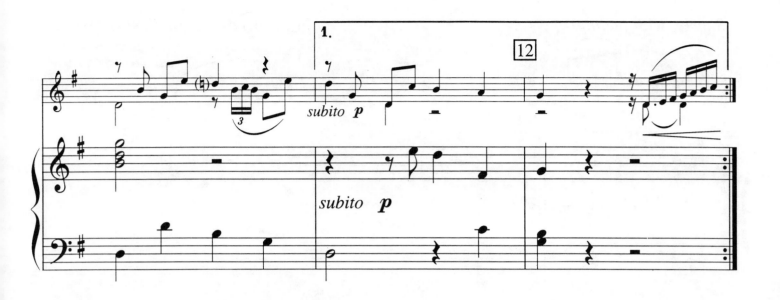

O Sole Mio

Slowly, with feeling

Eduardo di Capua (1864-1917)

William Tell Overture

from the opera "William Tell"

Gioacchino Rossini (1792-1868)